Ramesses The Great
Master of the World

Ramesses The Great
Master of the World

Photographs and text by
WILLIAM MacQUITTY

Foreword by T.G.H James of the British Museum

Crown Publishers Inc., New York

The Author

William MacQuitty is a Fellow of the Royal Geographical Society, a Fellow of the Royal Photographical Society of Great Britain and an Honorary MA of The Queen's University of Belfast.

As photographer and author he has produced a number of highly successful books—*Abu Simbel, Irish Gardens, Buddha, Great Botanical Gardens of the World, Princes of Jade, The World in Focus, Island of Isis, Our World in Colour, Tutankhamun: The Last Journey, The Wisdom of the Ancient Egyptians* and now *Ramesses the Great: Master of the World.* He was chosen by the Shah of Persia from photographers all over the world to illustrate *Persia, The Immortal Kingdom,* the volume commemorating the 2,500th anniversary of the founding of the kingdom of Persia.

This, his fifth book on Ancient Egypt, is the culmination of a life-time study of Egyptology and follows his current best-seller, *Tutankhamun: The Last Journey.*

Acknowledgements

I wish to thank Mr T. G. H. James, Keeper of Egyptian Antiquities, British Museum, who most kindly wrote the Foreword and checked my manuscript; he also supplied the translation of the hieroglyphs forming the names of Ramesses the Great.

My thanks also to the Oxford University Press for permission to print the quotations from Sir Alan Gardiner's *Egypt of the Pharaohs* which appear on pages 12, 24, 25 and 29.

On the fiftieth anniversary of my first visit to Egypt I give special thanks to my Egyptian friends, to H. E. Adel Taher, Under-Secretary of State in the Ministry of Tourism and to his Directors: Mr Aly Kahala in Aswan, Mr Galad Ead in Luxor, Mr Mohamed Ibrahim in Cairo, Mme Nadia Ibrahim in Alexandria and Mr Sami el Masri in London, who together with their courteous colleagues have been so helpful. My deepest gratitude to H.E. Dr Gamal ed-Din Mukhtar, formerly Under-Secretary of State in charge of the Antiquities Service, to H.E. Mr Samih Anwar, the Egyptian Ambassador in London, and to the Egyptian Exploration Society.

Finally I would like to thank Peter Wrigley and Roger Hearn, who designed and edited the book.

Front cover
The front cover shows a colossal head of Ramesses II in his temple at Luxor. He is wearing the double crown of Upper and Lower Egypt.

Title page
The temples of Abu Simbel had they not been moved would have been covered by the lake created by the new High Dam at Aswan. This picture shows them in their new site 200 feet above the old one and safe above the highest water level.

Right
The heads of Ramesses II cut from the façade of his temple at Abu Simbel wait to be reerected on the new site 200 feet higher up and 690 feet south of their original position. 1,050 blocks were skilfully removed from the mother rock to accomplish the splendid work of precision engineering required to move the temples.

Ramesses The Great
© Mitchell Beazley Publishers Ltd 1978
Text © William MacQuitty 1978
Photographs © William MacQuitty 1978
All rights reserved

Edited and designed by
Mitchell Beazley Publishers Ltd, London

First published in the United States of America in 1978 by
Crown Publishers, Inc.
One Park Avenue,
New York,
N.Y. 10016.

Library of Congress Cataloging in Publication Data

MacQuitty, William.
  Ramesses the Great.

  1. Rameses II, King of Egypt – Tomb.
2. Egypt – Antiquities. I. Title.
DT88.M3 1978   932.01   78–425
ISBN 0–517–53400–2 (Paperbound)
ISBN 0–517–53457–6 (Hardbound)

Printed in Spain by Printer industria gráfica s.a.,
Provenza, 388, 5.ª planta - Barcelona-25
Sant Vicenç dels Horts   1978
Depósito Legal B. 33459-1978
Phototypeset in England by Tradespools Ltd.,
Frome, Somerset.

Foreword

When the Ancient Egyptians who lived in the last centuries of pharaonic power looked back into their country's past for a figure of overwhelming stature they chose Ramesses II. By his buildings alone he was undoubtedly a man of exceptional achievement. The present-day visitor to Egypt ceases, by the end of his visit, to be surprised at the architectural presence of this king, when at almost every great site he has had the works of Ramesses pointed out by his eager guide. Ramesses has become almost synonymous with great construction. How much more in antiquity must those buildings, and others long perished, have spoken of the greatness of Usimare-Setpenre Ramesses. In ancient story he was the king under whom remarkable things occurred; even a relatively routine event like his marriage to a daughter of the Hittite king was romanticized in the tale of the Princess of Bakhtan. Ramesses was the Rampsinitus of Herodotus. His names were copied by his successors; they were used on scarabs made outside Egypt for generations after his death, as if they were in themselves magically endowed. Even today his cartouches are easily recognized by the tourist who has had one lesson in hieroglyphs, and thinks he has made a hieroglyphic breakthrough.

Yet, from close examination of surviving records it is surprisingly difficult to substantiate wholly this posthumous reputation. After the stirring events of his early years, Ramesses' reign was mostly quiet and peaceful. His dubious success at Kadesh was, however, the foundation of his greatness, for with conscious effort the story of that battle was used unashamedly to inflate the reputation of the king. The success of that piece of public relations is evident in all that has to do with Ramesses. And it persists until today. In the very act of writing this book William MacQuitty testifies to the continuing force of the legend. Through his brilliant photographs he, as surely, contributes to its continuation. In the long run legend is more durable than actual achievement. Ramesses certainly lives.

T. G. H. James
Keeper of the Department of Egyptian Antiquities,
British Museum, London

In the heart of Paris, in the Place de la Concorde, stands a magnificent obelisk. Its inscription reads: "Ramesses conqueror of all foreign peoples, master of all crown bearers, Ramesses who fought the millions bids the whole world subdue itself to his power upon the wish of his father Amun." Its twin still adorns the temple at Luxor, where Ramesses II, known as Ramesses the Great, worshipped Amun, the Imperial god of the Ancient Egyptians.

The events of the life of Ramesses II remain in large part a mystery, but from what we do know at least one personality trait emerges. Ramesses was never slow to record or glorify his achievements. We must conclude that, had Paris existed in his lifetime and had he conquered it, he would surely have placed just such an obelisk there himself.

The name Ramesses recurs in Egyptian history of the New Kingdom period (1567 BC to 1085 BC). In all 11 Ramesses reigned in the course of the Nineteenth and Twentieth Dynasties. Ramesses I founded the Nineteenth Dynasty in 1320 BC, Ramesses XI closed the Twentieth in 1085 BC.

The period of the New Kingdom was one of prosperity and power for Egypt. The pharaohs controlled a number of states on the margins of Egypt, exacting tribute and suppressing with force the inevitable periodic rebellions. The frequency with which major buildings were erected—the spate of building seems to have reached its peak under Ramesses II—is evidence of Egyptian prosperity. Power and prosperity apart, it was also a period of great religious change under the heretic Pharaoh Akhenaten, Ramesses II's predecessor on the throne by some hundred years.

The treasure of Tutankhamun's tomb is the richest ever found in Egypt—indeed, it is by the treasure that was buried with him that he is now remembered. This is the innermost of the three nesting coffins in which his mummy was laid. Made of solid 22-carat gold it weighs an incredible 296 lb troy.

Akhenaten decreed that only one god should be worshipped, Aten, the sun's disc, the source of all light and life on earth. His decree was no more popular with the people than it was with the priests, a body whose influence was to be reckoned with. It was not surprising then that on Akhenaten's death his successor, the young Tutankhamun, presided over a gradual abandonment of the cult of the new god and a reinstatement of the multitude of old gods. The period of change had lasted fewer than 20 years, but it left its scars.

Only 48 years separate the two pharaohs who are perhaps the best known: Tutankhamun and Ramesses II. They could hardly have been more different. Tutankhamun died at the age of 18, but his tomb contained the richest treasure known to the world. His mummy, although undisturbed until it was discovered in 1922, is in a poor state of preservation. He left no children. Ramesses on the other hand lived to the ripe old age of 97, but his tomb is a jagged, empty cavern robbed of its treasure, which might have surpassed that of Tutankhamun. His mummy suffered frequent moves, but is still in an excellent state of preservation for all the world to see, and he fathered an astounding 111 sons and 67 daughters. Tutankhamun left few marks other than his tomb; Ramesses was the most prolific builder of any age. Perhaps half the surviving temples in Egypt bear the marks of his handiwork and his name appears in nearly every group of ruins in the country.

On Tutankhamun's death the throne was taken over by Ay, a high priest who had been the power behind the young king. On his death four years

later Tutankhamun's general Horemheb became pharaoh and consolidated his rather slender claim to the throne by marrying Mutnedjmet, sister of the famous and beautiful Nefertiti, wife of Akhenaten. Horemheb was a strong ruler and rapidly set about removing all traces of Tutankhamun and the enlightened Akhenaten. He also destroyed totally the lovely city of Akhetaten, built by Akhenaten and dedicated to the sun's disc. After a reign of 28 years Horemheb was succeeded by his vizier, Pra'messe, whom we know as Ramesses I. Ramesses was a man of relatively humble origin whose father had been a captain in the army. He was already an old man when he came to the throne and his reign lasted less than two years. He was followed by Seti I, father of Ramesses the Great.

Seti I lacked royal blood, but he was a resourceful man and pleased the priests, who had not yet recovered from the injuries inflicted on them by Akhenaten, by restoring and rebuilding their temples. He also built a magnificent temple at Abydos, which was the reputed burial place of the god Osiris, who with his wife Isis and their son Horus formed the trinity of one of the most important cults in Ancient Egypt. In addition to helping to restore faith in the old gods Seti successfully defeated the Libyans, Hittites and Syrians, whose armies had penetrated the country along its northern frontiers. This great ruler reigned for 15 years and was buried in the largest tomb in the Valley of the Kings. It is cut 300 feet deep into the tawny limestone cliffs at Biban el-Moluk and the walls are richly decorated with scenes of the journey through the underworld.

Seti's achievement was indeed impressive. We know little of his relationship with his second son, the future Ramesses II, other than that the boy was given great responsibilities and great honours at a very early age. Seti had his son crowned with full ceremonial and it appears that Ramesses acted as co-regent with his father. We do know that by the time he was ten years old the future king was a captain in the army and had been given his own harem, but we do not know how Ramesses' elder brother was circumvented for the succession; Ramesses removed all trace of him from the record.

Ramesses' first proclamation, inscribed at Abydos, implies a co-regency; inscriptions in his temple at Karnak confirm the impression. The Abydos inscription reads:

"The universal lord himself magnified me whilst I was a child until I became ruler. He gave me the land while I was in the egg, the great ones smelling the earth before my face. When I was inducted as eldest son to be Hereditary Prince upon the throne of Geb [the earth god] I reported the state of the Two Lands as captain of the infantry and chariotry. Then when my father appeared in glory before the people, I being a babe in his lap, he said concerning me: 'Crown him as king that I may see his beauty whilst I am alive.' And he called to the chamberlains to fasten the crowns upon my forehead. 'Give him the Great One [the sacred asp] upon his head,' said he concerning me whilst he was on earth."

(translation by A. H. Gardiner)

Upon his accession in about 1290 BC Ramesses, just like many new kings, spent the first few years of his reign visiting his kingdom and the territories

Isis, wife of Osiris and mother of Horus, was one of the four "protector" goddesses, guarding and mourning the dead.

Osiris, god of the underworld, represented as a dead king. He was also venerated as a god of the flooding Nile.

Right
Nefertiti, Queen of Akhenaten, the heretic pharaoh, and one of the legendary beauties of Ancient Egypt. This unfinished carving comes from Tell el Amarna; it is now in the Cairo Museum.

Overleaf
A section of the ceiling of the burial chamber in the tomb of Seti I, Ramesses' father. It shows some of the gods as part of a heavenly constellation.

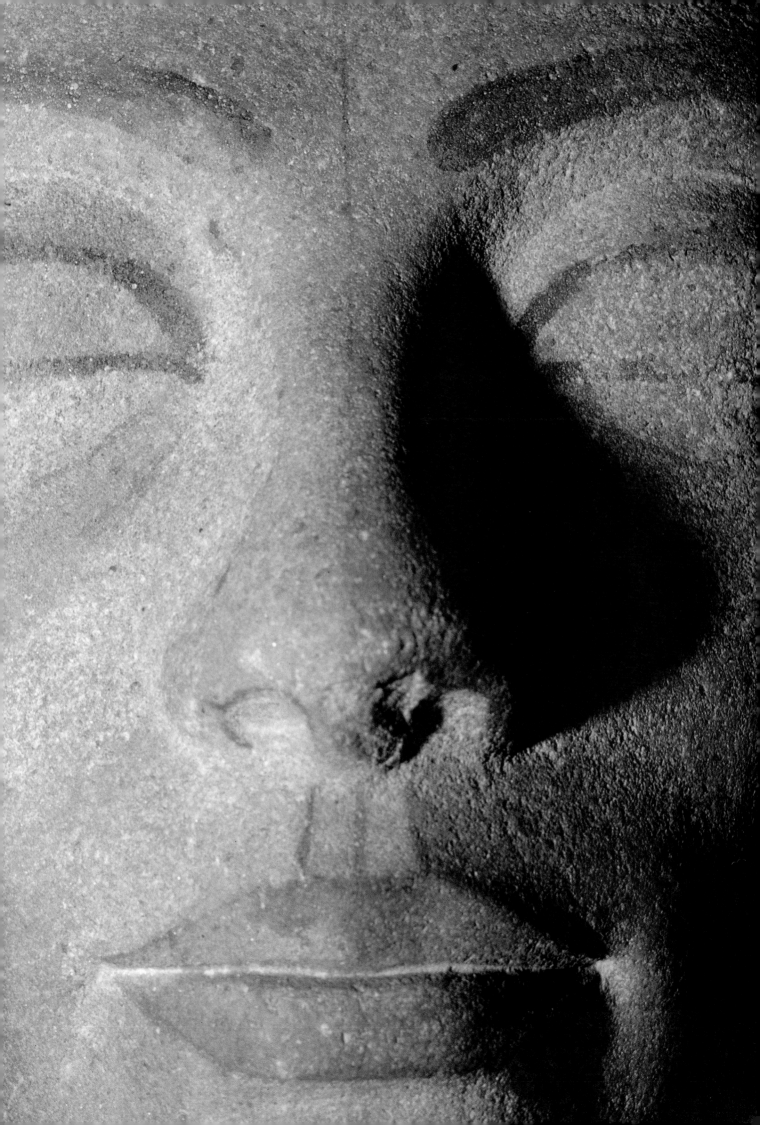

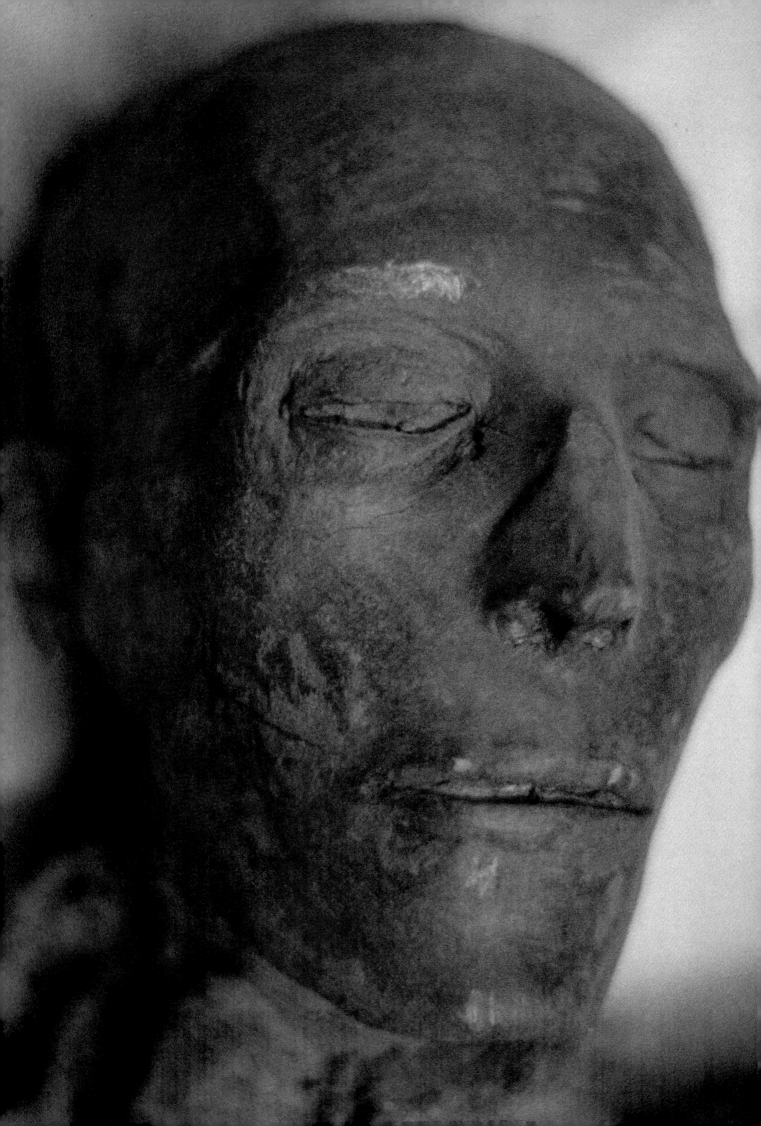

that owed him allegiance, instituting military expeditions against those parts of his empire that were troublesome and initiating the monumental building programmes that were to be a continuing feature of his reign.

Very early on it seems that he made an expedition to Nubia, and it was probably on this occasion that he set in motion the building of the famous temples at Abu Simbel. He chose a magnificent site where the Nile curved to form a delightful bay and the milky green waters lapped at the base of sandstone cliffs over 300 feet high; such a position is rare in the flat, arid desert through which the great river flows. His reason for building these remarkable temples was to demonstrate the power of the Egyptian Empire to a conquered country, for Nubia was at that stage a subject state. He was also able to portray himself in Nubia as an equal with the gods, a liberty he would not have been able to take at home in Egypt.

In the second year of his reign we know that the Nile delta was attacked by the "Sea Peoples", in the third that his first pylon or tower was finished at the temple of Luxor and that in the same year he mounted a military expedition to Palestine and Phoenicia, where he was apparently successful in pacifying the frontier between the Egyptian Empire and the Hittites.

The Hittites, together with the coalition of neighbouring states that they had built, were the only serious rivals to the power of Egypt. Seti I, Ramesses' father, had successfully subdued them for a while, but in the fifth year of his reign Ramesses was called upon to do likewise, in response to the news that the Hittite King Muwatallish was preparing once more to

Left
The well-preserved mummy of Seti I, which is now in Cairo Museum.

Overleaf
Part of the façade of Ramesses' temple at Abu Simbel, with the heads of the two northernmost statues, taken before the temple was moved to its new location.

Below
This wall painting from the tomb of Rekhmire at Sheikh abd el Qurna, shows Nubians bringing gifts of animals to Egypt. Nubia was a separate state at this time but part of the Egyptian Empire.

attack Egypt. Ramesses set out in the spring, crossed the Egyptian frontier at Sile and after four weeks' marching found himself some 15 miles from Kadesh. This fortified town, now Tel Neby Mend, lies in an angle formed by the river Orontes (now called Asi) and one of its small tributaries—a key position guarding the main route that any north- or south-bound army had to take. Ramesses' troops consisted of 500 two-man chariots, 8,000 spearmen and 9,000 others—18,000 in all. They were grouped in four divisions called after the gods Amun, Re, Ptah and Sutekh. Muwatallish, helped by surrounding tribes, had gathered together 20,000 men, including 2,500 three-man chariots.

Kadesh had been captured by Seti I, but had then fallen into Hittite hands and was therefore a special target for his son. After passing the night on a hilltop overlooking the town Ramesses set out at dawn leading the advance division of Amun down the hill and across the Orontes. As he waited for his long-drawn-out columns to catch up with him, prisoners were brought in who declared that the Hittites were still far away in the land of Khaleb, now Aleppo. Delighted by this information Ramesses pressed on with his bodyguard far ahead of the rest of his army and set up camp. While he was enjoying a meal in anticipation of a triumphant entry into Kadesh, two captured Hittite spies, after a severe beating, betrayed the fact that the entire army of Muwatallish lay hidden to the east of Kadesh, fully prepared.

Ramesses had barely time to reproach his officers and send messengers to hasten the arrival of his remaining divisions when the Hittites were upon

Right
One of the colossal statues of Ramesses on the façade of his temple at Abu Simbel. Beside him is a representation of Nefertari, upper left is a carving of "Horus of the Horizon", Re-Horakhty the sky god, son of Isis and Osiris, to whom the temple is dedicated.

Overleaf
Ramesses in his chariot wreaking havoc among rebellious Nubians. From a cast in the British Museum taken at the Temple of Luxor.

Below
A painting from the temple of Ramesses II at Beit el-Wali shows Nubians bringing tribute to Egypt.

him. They had passed to the south of the town, forded the river and poured down on the unprepared division of Re, which fled in utter confusion to the division of Amun. The forces of Amun were, however, in no better position to withstand the onslaught than the division of Re, and were further hindered by the panic of the fugitives; they too were swept away in a disastrous rout. The remaining two divisions, unaware of the fate of their fellows, were still proceeding slowly in the direction of Kadesh.

At this moment by all the laws of battle Ramesses was a beaten man. In fact this was his greatest hour. Calling for his chariot and horses and Menna, his shield-bearer, he flung himself into a series of headlong charges, which held the Hittite forces until his laggard legions appeared upon the scene and drove the Hittites from the field. The great battle is told in inscriptions in the temples of Abu Simbel, Karnak, Luxor, Abydos and the Ramesseum as well as in papyrus scrolls. The following translation is from *Egypt of the Pharaohs* by A. H. Gardiner:

"Then His Majesty started forth at a gallop, and entered into the host of the fallen ones of Khatti, being alone by himself, none other with him. And His Majesty went to look about him, and found surrounding him on his outer side 2,500 pairs of horses with all the champions of the fallen ones of Khatti and of the many countries who were with them, from Arzawa, Masa, Pidasa, Keshkesh, Arwen, Kizzuwadna, Khaleb, Ugarit, Kadesh, and Luka: they were three men to a pair of horses as a

A carving in Ramesses' temple at Abu Simbel, showing the Pharaoh in his chariot at the Battle of Kadesh. He is accompanied by a pet lion.

A granite carving of the sacred scarab at the temple of Karnak, where much of Ramesses' building activity was concentrated. The scarab, or dung-beetle, rolls its egg up in a ball of dung, on which the hatched young feeds. In Egyptian mythology the ball became a symbol of the sun, source of life, and the scarab the force which propelled it in the sky.

Overleaf
Paintings from the tomb at Deir-el-Medina of Senedjem, showing him and his wife Iyneferti, farming the heavenly fields.

unit, whereas there was no captain with me, no charioteer, no soldier of the army; my infantry and chariotry melted away before them, not one of them stood firm to fight with them. Then said His Majesty: 'What ails thee, my father Amun? Is it a father's part to ignore his son? Have I done anything without thee, do I not walk and halt at thy bidding? I have not disobeyed any course commanded by thee. How great is the great lord of Egypt to allow foreigners to draw nigh in his path! What careth thy heart, O Amun, for these Asiatics so vile and ignorant of God? Have I not made for thee my Mansion of Millions of Years and given thee all my wealth as a permanent possession and presented to thee all lands together to enrich thy offerings, and have caused to be sacrificed to thee tens of thousands of cattle and all manner of sweet-scented herbs? No good deeds have I left undone. . . . What will men say if even a little thing befall him who bends himself to thy counsel?'"

Fortified by his prayers to Amun, Ramesses rallied his shield-bearer, Menna, who not unnaturally was intimidated by the odds of 2,500 to 1. The account continues with Menna saying:

"'My good Lord, thou strong Ruler, thou great saviour of Egypt on the day of fighting, we stand alone in the midst of the battle. Behold, the infantry and chariotry have deserted us, for what reason dost thou

remain to rescue them? Let us get clear and do thou save us, O Usi-maresetpenre.' Then said His Majesty to his shield-bearer: 'Stand firm, steady thy heart, my shield-bearer. I will enter in among them like the pounce of a falcon, killing, slaughtering, and casting to the ground. What careth thy heart for these effeminate ones at millions of whom I take no pleasure?' Thereupon His Majesty started forth quickly and entered at a gallop into the midst of the battle for the sixth time of entering in amongst them."

Ramesses' bold attack saved the day. The advancing Hittite chariots had pursued the divisions of Re and Amun and were exhausted. Ramesses must have had some of his household troops, and under his headlong charges the spent forces of the Hittites were driven back to the river bank. Muwatallish, watching the battle from the eastern bank of the Orontes, inexplicably failed to throw in 8,000 spearmen whom he had in reserve.

The next day the severed hands of the slain were presented to Ramesses, and his troops were loud in their praises of their leader, but Ramesses reminded them that he had had to fight the enemy without their help and reserved his praises for his shield-bearer, Menna, and for his two horses, Victory in Thebes and Mut is Satisfied, which had carried him to victory. He gave orders that they should be fed in his presence at court.

The Battle of Kadesh could easily have been won by the Hittites if they had used all their forces. Ramesses' valiant charges would have been useless and the Egyptian forces annihilated. As it was, neither side won. Ramesses did not take Kadesh but returned home as rapidly as possible to relate the story of his great victory, which, in fact, was the story of his personal courage overcoming his bad generalship.

Ramesses' failure to take Kadesh cost him dear. This sign of Egyptian weakness prompted many of the petty states of Palestine and southern Syria to rebel against Egyptian overlordship. Not only did he have to mount campaigns against them, but of course the Hittites themselves were still eager to inflict significant defeats on their rival.

It was 16 years after the Battle of Kadesh, in the 21st year of Ramesses' reign, that Hittite–Egyptian hostility was resolved with a major peace treaty. The treaty's terms were remarkably modern: they included a mutual non-aggression pact, a mutual defence pact, reciprocal support to assure the succession of the legitimate heirs of either sovereign and even an extradition and asylum agreement. Identical copies of the treaty were discovered in Thebes, the Egyptian capital, and in Boghazköy, the capital of the Hittites a thousand miles away.

Twenty-nine years after the famous battle the treaty was further cemented by the marriage of the young daughter of the then Hittite King Khattusilis to Ramesses. The bride's arrival was the cause of great rejoicing, representatives of both nations eating and drinking together and "being at one heart like brothers, and there being no rancour". The maiden found favour in Ramesses' eyes and was raised to the position of being one of the King's great wives. One wonders how the other great wives felt about the new arrival, especially Queen Nefertari, who was undoubtedly his favourite.

Ramesses and Egypt were now secure in their imperial power and vast wealth and it is time to look at his lasting achievement—building. It is

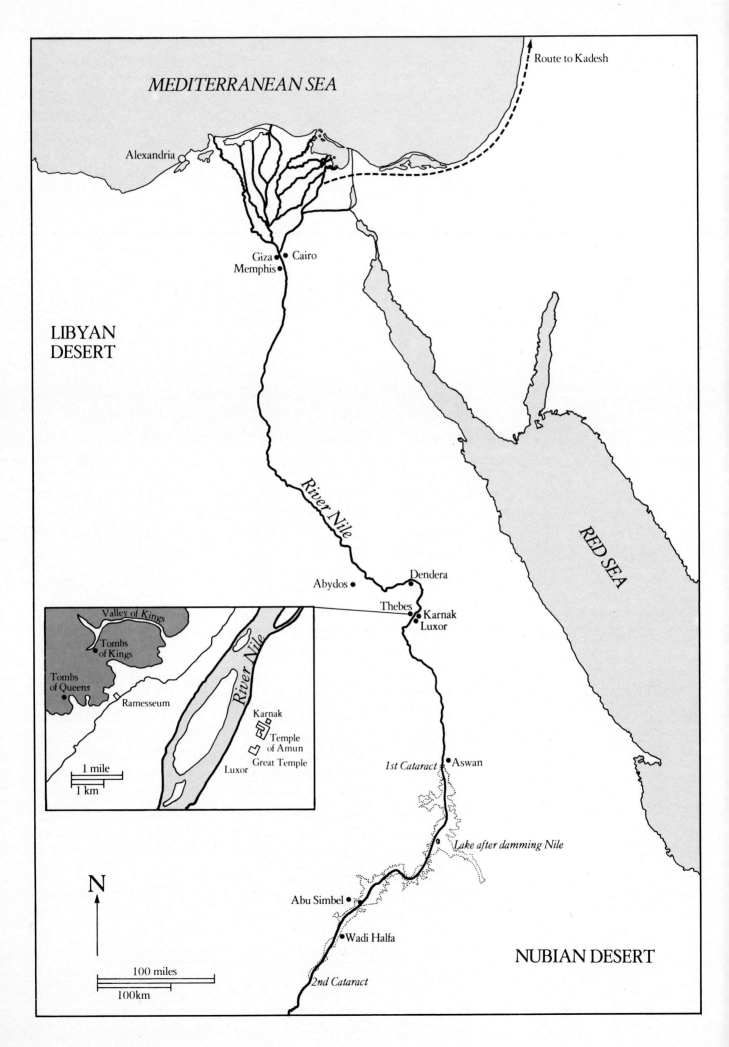

MEDITERRANEAN SEA

Route to Kadesh

Alexandria

LIBYAN
DESERT

Giza ● Cairo
Memphis ●

River Nile

RED SEA

Abydos ●

Dendera

Thebes
Karnak
Luxor

Valley of Kings
Tombs
of Kings
Tombs
of Queens
Ramesseum

River Nile

Karnak
Temple
of Amun
Luxor
Great Temple

1 mile
1 km

1st Cataract ● Aswan

Lake after damming Nile

N

Abu Simbel ●

Wadi Halfa ●

NUBIAN DESERT

100 miles
100km

2nd Cataract

Above

A representation of the last rites from the Book of the Dead of Hunefer. *The figure on the left, in the leopard skin, is the priest in charge of the ceremony. From the British Museum.*

impossible to appreciate why he committed such vast resources to temple-building without understanding something of the religion of which he, as a living god, was an integral part.

By the time Ramesses reached the throne the structure and organization of Egyptian religion had become very sophisticated. As Pharaoh, the god–king, he was the most powerful creature known to mankind; below him came the high priests and below them prophets, "servants of god" and ordinary priests, the "pure ones". In addition there were officials, scribes, police, craftsmen and labourers, who, although their livelihood depended on the temple, were laymen. Each temple was a miniature town and included women whose job was to sing and shake the sacred *sistra*, a form of rattle, during the services. There were also women of a higher position known as "divine wives of the god".

The daily rites performed in the temples in the name of Ramesses were conducted in the inner shrine in secret. Ideally these rituals should have been carried out by the Pharaoh, but as this was impossible he appointed priestly deputies, except perhaps for ceremonies on the principal feast days.

The ritual varied little: first the officiating priest purified himself in the sacred pool, which was part of each temple complex. Next he lit a censer of charcoal on which he placed incense to purify and scent the area through which he passed. At the sacred shrine he broke the clay seal and opened the doors to reveal the divine image of the god. He then prostrated himself before it, chanting hymns of adoration. Next he offered the god the figure of

Maet, goddess of Truth, and a symbol of the Eye of Horus—still to be seen on the bows of Mediterranean fishing boats. The god, now endowed with life, was taken from its shrine and washed and dressed again as if it were a living deity. It was then replaced in the shrine, offered food, and finally the shrine was sealed up until the following morning.

In return for these attentions the god granted Ramesses life on earth and, more important, union with the god and eternal future happiness. The public were excluded from these ceremonies, but were content to know that Ramesses enjoyed the favour of the gods and that all manner of blessings would in consequence descend upon them. They had little contact with the great gods and goddesses, but followed smaller cults and magical practices of their own.

The wealth of the temples was considerable. Karnak, Ramesses' chief temple, eventually covered 60 acres and could easily accommodate ten European cathedrals. It possessed 700 acres of land, 81,000 slaves, 400,000 head of cattle and 83 ships and had an enormous annual income of gold, silver, copper, food, drink and clothing, in fact everything necessary for the well-being of its devoted servants. In the reign of Ramesses III, a tenth of all the best land of Egypt was in the hands of the temples. Via the wealth of the temples and the power of the priests Ramesses had complete authority over his subjects. The power of the priests lay in their ability to provide comfort on earth and everlasting life in the world to come for those who obeyed their teaching and made appropriate gifts to the temples.

The requirements for life after death had a compelling logic. The gods must be honoured and the law obeyed so that the deceased could pass the tests put to him in the Hall of Justice in the presence of Osiris the King of the Underworld. Standing in front of each of the 42 terrible assessors the deceased had to state that he had not committed the sin for which that particular assessor had the authority to punish. This statement was the famous "Negative Confession", which embodied the moral code of the Ancient Egyptians. It consisted of a series of denials—I have not spoken falsely, I have not killed, I have not given short measure, and so on. During this time the deceased's heart was being weighed in a large balance against Truth, represented by a feather, and if found wanting it was devoured by a terrible creature, Amemit, a mixture of crocodile, leopard and hippopotamus.

The Osiris myth occurs frequently and probably has some historic truth. Osiris, a liberal ruler, was killed by his brother Seth, who cut up his body and scattered the pieces. Isis, the wife of Osiris, found the pieces and Re the sun-god sent down his son Anubis to wrap the body in bandages like those of a mummy. Isis beat her wings and caused breath to enter the corpse until Osiris miraculously lived and moved again. Unable to return as an earthly king, Osiris reigned in the spirit world as god of the dead. Every Egyptian believed that because Osiris had risen from the dead he too could achieve the same destiny provided the requirements of religion were duly satisfied.

Because of this certainty of life after death, the Egyptians decorated their tombs in a non-funereal way. There is no atmosphere of death or sadness

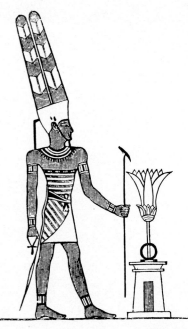

Amun, the great god of Thebes.

Below
Since the after-life was to be looked forward to, feasting and dancing were often portrayed in tombs. From Thebes.

Anubis, the jackal god, patron deity of embalmers.

Below
These inscriptions hammered on a rock face at Siheil, an island at the beginning of the First Cataract, were put there by high officials as invocations of the Gods of the Cataract.

in them, rather a feeling of sympathy for the dead, a feeling that in some way we have shared their hopes and fears and in thinking about them have given them a moment of life. The tombs of the kings and queens were devoted to paintings and carvings of a religious nature, but the tombs of the nobles and lesser mortals show their way of life in glowing colours and vivid action. Even after 3,000 years the scenes are as fresh and new as if they had only just been completed.

The central notion of rebirth and of the cycles of life in part arose from—and was annually reinforced by—the two great elemental forces that sustained life in Ancient Egypt: the sun and the Nile. Each night the Egyptian sun dies in a blaze of glory in the western desert, each morning it rises triumphantly in the east. The Egyptians were a life-loving people, and the idea of death being the end of everything was as abhorrent to them as it is to most of humanity. The conviction grew that just as the sun died every night and rose every morning so too could man, provided certain rituals were observed.

The Nile's cycle is of course annual. Without it Egypt would have been a sandy wasteland. Where the waters flowed the yellow desert was covered with rich silt and sprang into bloom. The annual flow controlled not just the prosperity but the very life of the country; and Ramesses expressed his, the god–king's, relationship to the river in religious terms.

Ramesses' building programmes then were an expression of his own grandeur, but not just as a secular ruler. He was a living god paying tribute

to the other deities as well as to himself. In his building he was fortunate in having the finest masons and they were fortunate in having an abundant supply of materials. Perhaps their greatest achievement was the cutting of huge statues and obelisks weighing a thousand tons from the living granite with only primitive tools of stone and copper. The carving on the polished surface of these huge monuments rivals the best work done today. The method for removing these vast masses is clearly shown in the Aswan quarries. One monster, still partly attached to its bedrock, is 138 feet long and would have weighed 1,168 tons. The shape of the obelisk was roughly cut out by pounding a channel round it with lumps of green dolerite, a stone harder than granite. To separate the mass from the mother rock it is possible that the masons cut slots in the underside and into them hammered sycamore wedges. The wedges were then soaked in water and the resultant expansion split the rock along the line chosen. Seven months seems to have been the time it took to carve out one large obelisk.

The skill of the masons was equalled by the engineers, who with only wood and rope to help them transported these vast masses to sites all over Egypt. First a path was cleared from the quarry to the river bank and then, using wooden sleds and rollers, an army of men assisted by teams of oxen dragged the monuments to the water's edge, where they loaded their burdens into barges. The heavily laden barges sailed to their destination assisted by the flow of the river. Use was also made of the inundation, which enabled the barges to proceed over the flooded land and deposit their loads far from

Previous page
An unfinished carving, possibly an Osiride statue of Ramesses II, in the quarries at Aswan. The lower part has not been cut from the underlying granite.

Below
A huge obelisk partly cut from the rose-red granite of Aswan. A flaw was revealed during the work and so the task of lifting the monument was abandoned. Had this fault not occurred it would have been the largest single stone monument in the world, measuring 138 feet long, 14 feet square at the base and weighing 1,168 tons.

the river banks. The huge stones used for building the pyramids were transported in this way.

After the monument reached its destination came the superhuman task of erecting it on its prepared site base. No exact information is available as to how this was done, but one plausible explanation suggests that a mound of earth was raised round the base stone up to approximately half the height of the obelisk with an earth ramp leading up to it. The hollow centre was half-filled with sand and the obelisk was then hauled up the ramp and tipped in. The sand was gradually removed through a small tunnel at the bottom, causing the monument to settle down slowly until with the aid of ropes and levers it came to rest on its base. The ramp and mound were now removed; the seemingly impossible had been achieved. The largest statue in the world ever to have been hewn out of a single piece of granite was transported in this way and set up in the Ramesseum, the funerary temple of Ramesses the Great on the west bank of the Nile at Luxor. Unfortunately, possibly due to an earthquake, it eventually crashed to the ground. Shelley immortalized this fallen colossus:

The fallen colossal statue of Ramesses II in his funerary temple, the Ramesseum, at Thebes. It was here that commemorative rites were performed for the dead Pharaoh. This was the statue which inspired Shelley's poem "Ozymandias".

"I met a traveller from an antique land
Who said: 'Two vast and trunkless legs of stone
Stand in the desert. . . . Near them, on the sand,
Half sunk, a shattered visage lies, whose frown,
And wrinkled lip and sneer of cold command,

Tell that its sculptor well those passions read
Which yet survive, stamped on these lifeless things,
The hand that mocked them, and the heart that fed.
And on the pedestal these words appear:
"My name is Ozymandias, king of kings:
Look on my works, ye Mighty, and despair!"
Nothing beside remains. Round the decay
of that colossal wreck, boundless and bare,
The lone and level sands stretch far away.' "

Ozymandias is the Greek interpretation of the prenomen of Ramesses "Usermaat-re", "Powerful of Truth is Re", the sun-god of Heliopolis.

Of all the buildings of Ramesses Karnak must take pride of place. Its Hypostyle Hall, which Ramesses completed, is regarded by Baedeker as one of the wonders of the world. Its vast roof is supported by 134 columns and covers an area of 6,000 square yards, spacious enough to accommodate the entire cathedral of Notre Dame in Paris. The columns are arranged in 16 rows, the largest ones in the centre being 12 feet in diameter—as thick as the Vendôme Column in Paris or Trajan's Column in Rome. Of the roof which they once supported (hypostyle = pillared) only the cross beams remain, great stones 25 feet long bridging the space between the pillars. The surface is covered with deeply incised carvings, some with traces of the original colour, a vast stone canvas portraying incidents in the lives of

Previous page
A view of the temple of Karnak showing the forecourt leading to the vast Hypostyle (pillared) Hall.

Right
The entrance to the great Hypostyle Hall at Karnak. The 16 huge central pillars are each 12 feet in diameter.

Below
Part of the avenue of ram-headed sphinxes at Karnak, set up by Ramesses II.

Ramesses and his father, their battles and conquests, their work and worship. The contrast between the sun-drenched forecourt and the mysterious interior of the Hypostyle Hall must have had a powerful effect on those of the populace who were permitted to enter. As they proceeded deeper into the temple they would have found the levels of the floors rising, the ceilings becoming lower and the light dwindling, until in the sanctuary which housed the god darkness was complete.

Ramesses paid tribute to his daughter–wife Nefertari—her name means "Beautiful Companion"—in stone on countless occasions. Nowhere, though, unless it be at Abu Simbel, did she receive greater homage than in her tomb. It is the finest in the Valley of Queens. The white stucco walls are covered with colourful paintings of the gods and picture writing from the *Book of the Dead*. The outlines of the paintings are clear and decisive. The atmosphere is feminine; Nefertari appears in tightly sheathed dresses, wearing beautiful jewellery round her slender neck and arms.

On the wall to the right of the entrance she worships Osiris; on the left her Ka, or spiritual double, plays a game and farther on adores the rising sun, which appears between two lions, Yesterday and Tomorrow. The mural continues with a blue crane and two hawks representing Isis and Nephthys watching the bier of Osiris, the symbol of resurrection. Here in the wall a doorway opens on to a steep stairway leading down to the burial hall. Above the doorway are the four sons of Horus—Imseti (human-headed), Hapi (ape-headed), Duamutef (jackal-headed), and Qebehsenuef (falcon-headed)—who are closely associated with the four goddesses who guard the organs kept in jars after their removal prior to mummification. On either side of the stairway the long triangles formed by the sloping roof are filled with pictures, which adorn the available space with great elegance. On the right the queen makes an offering to Hathor. On the opposite triangle she offers two bowls of wine to Isis, behind whom sits Nephthys, sister of Osiris. In the narrowest part of the triangles Maet, goddess of truth, sits with her wings before her.

The bottom of the stairs leads into the burial hall, the roof of which is supported by four square pillars, with a sunken area between them where once stood the sarcophagus. Here the work has been damaged by a moist, salty exudate coming through the plaster, and because of this the tomb has not been opened for many years. The sanctuary of the tomb is in the rear wall and is sadly spoilt; only fragments of the painting can be seen.

The tomb of Ramesses, by contrast, is alas an empty shell, but 300 miles to the south lies his greatest work: the rock temples of Abu Simbel. These are not funerary temples but monuments marking his southern territory, displaying his power to the Nubians. Looking at these massive and imposing statues it is easy to imagine the fear and respect they produced. They were rediscovered by Burckhardt in 1812, but at that time only one head was visible, the rest of the monuments being covered with fine sand which drifted in from the desert. This had protected them from natural erosion and perhaps more importantly from the fanatical fury of the Copts, who with hammers and chisels sought for generations to obliterate all evidence of the "idolatrous past".

In the past the temples could be reached by desert trails from Wadi Halfa and by boat across the Nile from the village directly opposite the temples.

Right
The burial chamber of the tomb of Seti I, the largest in the Valley of Kings. A detail from the ceiling is shown on pp. 14–15.

Overleaf
A detail from the wall paintings in the tomb of Senedjem (see also the agricultural scenes on pp. 26–27). It shows Osiris, god of the underworld, carrying the crook and flail, symbols of regal authority.

Today Wadi Halfa and the village lie 200 feet beneath the lake formed by the High Dam. The temples have been moved, but they still stand by the waters of the Nile, no longer milky green but azure blue, for the silt which produced the colour *eau de nil* has fallen to the bottom of the now still water.

The temples should be visited just before sunrise, when they are still hidden in the darkness of the western sky. As the pre-dawn lightens the black doorway emerges from the cliff followed on either side by the colossal figures of Ramesses. Suddenly the tip of the sun's disc appears above the horizon, its first rays light up a row of dog-faced baboons who line the top cornice of the temple, their paws raised in worship of the rising sun. These "Watchers for the Dawn" inform the Pharaoh that the sun-god has safely risen after his passage in his celestial barque through the waters of the underworld. Inside the temple eight huge statues of Ramesses wait for the light as they have for over 3,000 years. As the sun continues to rise it enters the temple and bathes the interior in a soft yellow light reflected from the sandstone floor. Beyond the eight statues lies a second chamber and beyond that a small antechamber leading to the sanctuary, 180 feet deep in the heart of the rock. Only on two days each year, the 23rd of February and the 23rd of October, do the rays shine directly on the four gods in the inner sanctuary. Here on one massive throne Ptah, Amen-Re, Ramesses II and Re-Horakhty sit in equal splendour.

In the antechamber stands a pedestal for the sacred barque of Amun, in which the image of the god was carried at religious celebrations. Made of

Above
Three statues of Ramesses with the attributes of Osiris. These Osiride figures stand in the entrance hall of Ramesses' temple at Abu Simbel.

Right
The southernmost of the three surviving colossi of Ramesses on the façade of his temple at Abu Simbel. The figures at the top of the building are carvings of dog-faced baboons, the "Watchers for the Dawn".

wood and not dissimilar in construction to the felucca, the sacred boat has not withstood the passage of time. Beside the seated figures of the gods the walls of the sanctuary teem with life. The low-relief sculpture still bears traces of the stone-ground colours, blue, orange, red and green. Many shades are delicately revealed in the reflected light, which carves dark shadows in the deeply etched reliefs. The work becomes progressively stronger as one leaves the inner chamber, as if the artists did not wish to linger near the gods, or perhaps the atmosphere became too suffocating for their best work. The temple is solid and impressive; the sandstone ceilings supported by rock pillars look as if they will stand for eternity. Everywhere there is a feeling of immense strength. Every inch of the rock surface is covered with lively carvings, most of them coloured, a flowing tapestry in stone, not only of life in the next world but of the exploits of Ramesses on earth. Moving from the sanctuary outwards through the small antechamber, the worn sandstone floor leads to the smaller hall whose ceiling is supported by four square pillars carved with sculptures of Ramesses and the gods. He makes offerings to Isis, Min, the god of fertility, and himself; he is content that his living self should worship his deified self. On the walls, accompanied by Nefertari, he makes offerings to the sacred barque of Amun carried on the shoulders of the priests.

As the sun continues to rise the light retreats across the sandy floor leading to the great entrance hall, 54 feet broad and 58 feet deep. The eight huge figures of Ramesses, sharply picked out against the light, make an even more impressive sight this way round than they do from the entrance. The figures on the south side wear the white crown of Upper Egypt and those on the north the double crown of Upper and Lower Egypt. They stand 30 feet high and their presence is overpowering. The other three sides of the columns from which they are carved show Ramesses with the gods Horus, Atum, Thoth, Min, Khnum, Amun-Re, Ptah, Re-Horakhty, Hathor, Isis and two Cataract goddesses, Satet and Anukis. Ramesses makes offerings, dances and holds hands with them in a union of friends.

Round the walls stretches the great historical pageant of his battle of Kadesh. All is depicted—the city of Kadesh, the marching infantry, the charging chariots, the triumph of Ramesses, the bound prisoners, his pet lion running beside his chariot, the counting of the hands of the slain, Ramesses smiting the foe, the hand-to-hand fighting—history's first memoirs of a victorious leader. As the sun rises further its light withdraws from the temple and the colour and the movement are lost in darkness until tomorrow's sunrise calls them once more to life. Outside, the expressions on the giant faces have become gentler, the sun now shines down upon them, highlighting them against the shadow of the rock face.

The width of the temple is 120 feet and the height 100, the seated colossi are 65 feet high and 25 feet across the shoulders. More important than size is the gentle serenity and warmth which they exude, an atmosphere of endless patience as they calmly await each new dawn. They have seen calamity, too: some 50 years after their completion Seti II had to repair the second colossus from the north; years later the head of the third colossus fell to the ground. The leg of this colossus bears a Greek inscription written in the Twenty-sixth Dynasty (664–525 BC): "The army of King Psammetichus, son of Theocles, passed this way and went on by Cercis as far as

the river permitted." Since then many lesser mortals hoping for immortality have left their names on the monument.

Nefertari appears three times on the façade of Ramesses' temple, as do several of the children, including one of his 111 sons, Amen(hir)khopshef, and the King's mother, Queen Mut-Tuy. The entrance is adorned with carvings of captive Asians and Negroes, arms pinioned behind their backs.

The smaller temple of Nefertari lies 150 yards north of her husband's and is 92 feet wide and 39 feet high. There are four statues of Ramesses and two of Nefertari standing between those of her husband. She wears a diaphanous garment with her hair framing her face and stopping just above her breasts. Round the royal legs their knee-high children shelter. The inscription on the buttresses inform the world that "His Majesty ordered the making of a temple in Ta-Seti (Nubia), cut into the mountain; the like has not been seen before—except for the son of Amun (i.e. Ramesses)."

The entrance hall has six pillars supporting the ceiling. They are decorated with heads of Hathor, the goddess of joy and lovemaking. Nefertari appears in a beautiful pose on the rear wall between Hathor and Mut. In the ante-chamber Ramesses and Nefertari are shown before Hathor and Isis. Inside the sanctuary Ramesses stands before his deified self and a deified Nefertari. In a niche in the rear wall Hathor emerges from the rock and beneath her Ramesses claims divine protection. The figures are badly mutilated and it seems that this part of the temple was never completed. Uncarved blank spaces in the walls were left by the masons for doorways into side chambers

Right
Falcon-headed Re-Horakhty with Hathor shown as a lady with the symbol of the West on her head; from a painting in Nefertari's tomb.

Below
The tomb of Nefertari, showing the Queen associated with various deities.

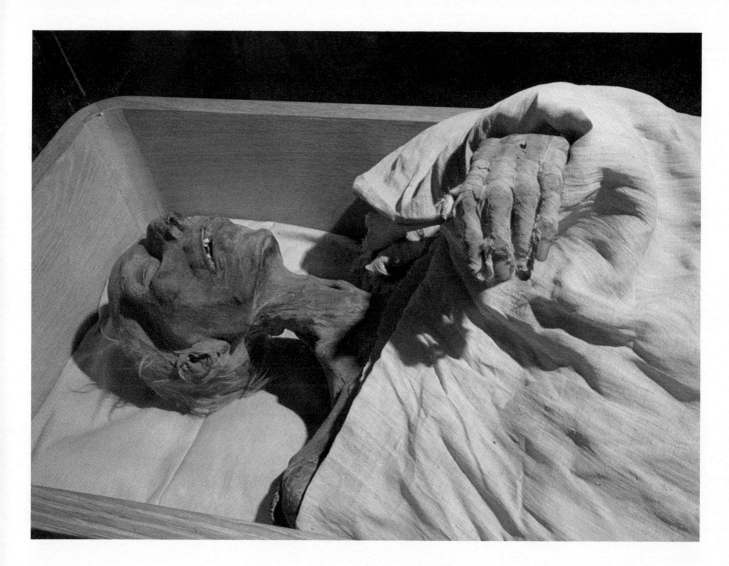

that were never excavated. Perhaps Ramesses thought he had done enough to immortalize his favourite wife.

Seven hundred miles to the north in the largest city in Africa stands the famous Cairo Museum. In the heart of this unique treasure-house surrounded by the priceless works of the past lies the mummy of Ramesses the Great. His wanderings have ended in a setting he could hardly have bettered. Here in a plain wooden coffin lie the remains of this great Pharaoh. Around him the royal mummies, including that of his son Merneptah, wait peacefully for the day of resurrection. Ramesses' head is uncovered and well poised on the slender neck. The chin and mouth are firm, the nose high, arched and commanding, the eyelids closed. Locks of light brown hair frame his head. It is a strong, arrogant face showing little sign of his 97 years. It is a face that has weathered 3,000 years and received perhaps even more homage after death than it did in life.

There is a saying in Ancient Egypt that to speak of the dead is to make them live again. Ramesses the Great is today more widely known than he ever was, even at the height of his immense power. This very human man, who like so many of us wanted to be remembered, has undoubtedly achieved his wish. We mortals of this anxious and uncertain age may well wonder if the work of our time is destined to survive as long as his.

"My name is Ozymandias, king of kings:
Look on my works, ye Mighty, and despair!"

Chronological Table

Including the names of the principal kings

Early Dynastic Period
First Dynasty (c. 3100–2890 BC)
Narmer (Menes)
Aha
Djer
Den
Semerkhet
Qaa
Second Dynasty (c. 2890–2686 BC)
Hotepsekhemwy
Nynetjer
Peribsen
Khasekhemwy

Old Kingdom
Third Dynasty (c. 2686–2613 BC)
Sanakhte
Djoser (Zoser)
Sekhemkhet
Huni
Fourth Dynasty (c. 2613–2494 BC)
Sneferu
Cheops
Chephren
Mycerinus
Fifth Dynasty (c . 2494–2345 BC)
Userkaf
Sahure
Nyuserre
Unas
Sixth Dynasty (c. 2345–2181 BC)
Teti
Pepi I
Merenre
Pepi II

First Intermediate Period
A time of political instability lasting from about 2181 BC to about 2133 BC including the Seventh to Tenth Dynasties, the order and names of whose kings are not fully established.

Middle Kingdom
Eleventh Dynasty (c. 2133–1991 BC)
Mentuhotpe I
Inyotef I–III
Mentuhotpe II–IV
Twelfth Dynasty (c. 1991–1786 BC)
Ammenemes I 1991–1962 BC
Sesostris I, 1971–1928 BC
Sesostris III, 1878–1843 BC
Ammenemes III, 1842–1797 BC
Thirteenth Dynasty (c. 1786–1633 BC)
Sebekhotpe III
Neferhotep

Second Intermediate Period
A further time of political instability during which Egypt was ruled in part by the Asiatic Hyksos. The Fourteenth and Sixteenth Dynasties are particularly shadowy, the former consisting of native rulers, and the latter of minor Hyksos.
Fifteenth (Hyksos) Dynasty (c. 1674–1567 BC)
Sheshi
Khyan
Apophis I
Apophis II
Seventeenth Dynasty (c. 1650–1567 BC)
Seqenenre
Kamose

New Kingdom
Eighteenth Dynasty (c. 1567–1320 BC)
Amosis, 1570–1546 BC
Amenophis I, 1546–1526 BC
Tuthmosis I, 1525–1512 BC
Tuthmosis II, 1512–1504 BC
Hatshepsut, 1503–1482 BC
Tuthmosis III, 1504–1450 BC
Amenophis II, 1450–1425 BC
Tuthmosis IV, 1425–1417 BC
Amenophis III, 1417–1379 BC
Akhenaten, 1379–1362 BC
Smenkhkare, 1364–1361 BC
Tutankhamun, 1361–1352 BC
Ay, 1352–1348 BC
Horemheb, 1348–1320 BC

Nineteenth Dynasty (c. 1320–1200 BC)
Ramesses I, 1320–1318 BC
Seti I, 1318–1304 BC
Ramesses II, 1304–1237 BC
Merneptah, 1236–1223 BC
Amenmesses, 1222–1217 BC
Seti II, 1216–1210 BC
Twentieth Dynasty (c. 1200–1085 BC)
Sethnakhte, 1200–1198 BC
Ramesses III, 1198–1166 BC
Ramesses IV–XI, 1166–1085 BC

Late New Kingdom
From the twenty-first to the beginning of the Twenty-fifth Dynasties (c. 1085–750 BC), Egypt was in political decline. The Twenty-fourth Dynasty was concurrent with the beginning of the Twenty-fifth Dynasty.

Late Period
Twenty-fifth Dynasty (c. 750–656 BC)
Piankhi, 750–716 BC
Shabaka, 716–695 BC
Taharqa, 689–664 BC
Twenty-sixth Dynasty (c. 664–525 BC)
Psammetichus I, 664–610 BC
Necho II, 610–595 BC
Apries, 589–570 BC
Amasis, 570–526 BC
The Twenty-seventh Dynasty consisted of Persian conquering kings, and the Twenty-eighth to Thirtieth Dynasties of the last native Egyptian rulers. In 332 BC Alexander the Great conquered Egypt, and thereafter the land was ruled first by Macedonian Greeks (the Ptolemies) and then as part of the Roman Empire.

Right
The god Horus, represented as a falcon, from his temple at Edfu.

The Names of Ramesses II

Ramesses II, like most Egyptian kings, possessed a long series of names and epithets of which two had special importance. These were the names placed inside cartouches—ovals that originally represented loops of rope with ties, probably signifying in a graphic manner that the king ruled "all that the sun encircled".

The first cartouche of Ramesses II, containing a name that is sometimes called the prenomen, reads "One powerful of Truth is Re, he whom Re has chosen"; in Egyptian it may have sounded something like Usimare-Setpenre. Egyptian texts could be written monumentally from left to right, or from right to left, and horizontally or vertically. Here the names are written to be read from left to right in order to fit in with the direction of English. The breakdown of the signs in this first name is as follows: ⊙ is the sun-disc, representing the god Re; ⸮, a ritual staff with a jackal head, with the phonetic value W + S + R, is a verb meaning "be powerful"; ⸮ is a figure of Maet, the goddess of Truth; ⊙ , the sun-disc again; ⸮, an adze with block of wood, with the phonetic value S + T + P, a verb meaning "choose", which, in combination with the sign 〜〜〜 (a ripple of water, of phonetic value N), represents here a special verb form. The precedence given to the sign ⊙ in both parts of the name is a graphic peculiarity of hieroglyphic writing which required that prominence be given to divine names in certain contexts.

The second cartouche of Ramesses II also contains a double name, often called the nomen: it can be translated "One beloved of Amun, one born of Re"—in Egyptian pronounced possibly Miamun-Ramessu. The signs of which the name is composed are the following: first, three signs "spelling" out the name of the god Amun— ⸮, the reed-leaf, with a phonetic value close to A; ⸮ , a gaming board with pieces in position, having the phonetic value M + N; and the water sign 〜〜〜 , of phonetic value N, here used to complement the N implicit in ⸮ ; then comes ⸮ , an irrigation channel of phonetic value M + R, here representing a form of the verb "love". The second part of the name, which can be seen to be the origin of Ramesses, consists of ⸮ , a seated divine falcon with a sun-disc on its head, representing Re; ⸮ , three foxes' skins tied together, of phonetic value M + S, here being a form of the verb "bear"; ⸮ , a door-bolt, with value S, representing a pronominal form.

The order and choice of signs used in writing these names are capable of great variation; thus the forms of the names discussed here represent only one set of possibilities.

Further Reading

Černy, J., *Ancient Egyptian Religion*, London, 1952

Edwards, A. B., *A Thousand Miles up the Nile*, London, 1877

Fraser, *Ptolemaic Alexandria*, 3 vols., Oxford, 1972

Gardiner, A. H., *The Kadesh Inscriptions of Ramesses II*, Oxford, 1960

——, *Egypt of the Pharaohs*, Oxford, 1961

General Introductory Guide to the Egyptian Collections in the British Museum, A,
   London, 1964

Iversen, Erik, *Obelisks in Exile I: The Obelisks of Rome*; *Obelisks in Exile II:*
   The Obelisks of Istanbul and England, Copenhagen, 1968 and 1972

James, T. G. H., *Myths and Legends of Ancient Egypt*, Hamlyn, 1969

——, *Archaeology of Ancient Egypt*, Bodley Head, 1972

Kees, H., *Ancient Egypt, A Cultural Topography*, London, 1961

MacQuitty, William, *Abu Simbel*, London, 1965

——, *Tutankhamun: The Last Journey*, London, 1972

——, *Island of Isis*, London, 1976

——, *The Wisdom of the Ancient Egyptians*, London, 1978

Montel, P., *Everyday Life in the Days of Ramesses the Great*, London, 1958

Cambridge Ancient History, 3rd ed., vol. II, part 2, Cambridge, 1975

Morenz, Siegfried, *Egyptian Religion*, London, 1973

Posener, G. (ed.), *A Dictionary of Egyptian Civilization*, London, 1962

Schmidt, J. D., *Ramesses II*, Baltimore, 1973

The prenomen of Ramesses II carved inside a representation of a loop of rope with the ends tied together, possibly signifying that the Pharaoh ruled over all "that the sun encircled". From Abu Simbel.

The back cover shows Ramesses smiting Nubian prisoners; a scene from his temple at Abu Simbel.